PRAISE FOR BRIGHT HOPE

"I knew Erin Cushman's new 28-day devotional book was going to be a great help as soon as I read the transparent, sobering first sentence on Day 1—"Grief makes us desperate." Each day's devotional entry offers a simple truth as nourishment for the mourning soul, then encourages quiet reflection. Biblical, life giving, and unrushed, which is what grieving hearts need. I highly commend it."

Dr. Andy Snider, *Lead Pastor, Radiant Church Austin.*

"Erin's personal experience with grief, as well as her long, faithful ministry with Hope Mommies, make her a trustworthy companion for anyone wading through sorrow and loss. The empathy, biblical truth, and resources found within these pages will anchor and nourish you, pointing you to the God of all comfort."

Caroline Cobb, *singer-songwriter.*

"Grief is not processed in a tidy set of steps. While different people grieve differently *Bright Hope* points to the one thing that is constant. Going through grief with Christ and in community makes it more bearable. I love the theme 'come to God as you are'. Erin knows the wisdom and comfort of obeying that invitation. I encourage those who are weary, grieving, and going through a tough season to read, meditate, and reflect on this life-giving devotional."

Dr. Garrett Higbee, *Pastor of Biblical Soul Care at Harvest Church; President of Soul Care Consulting; Leader Care Specialist for the Great Commission Collective.*

D0104618

"Erin's story and words give us all a courageous offering of hope in the darkness of grief and unanswered questions."
Sandra McCracken, *singer-songwriter.*

"This devotional is a 28-day journey with Jesus – offering His clear, comforting, concrete counsel. *Bright Hope* extends authentic, poignant, and biblical guidance – a foundation of truth amidst the tumultuous feelings of grief. May your journey through this devotional provide an anchor of hope through whatever your personal valley of the shadow of death may be."
Autumn Williams, *Director of UPPERROOM Global.*

"When grieving, what you truly need above all else is to encounter the living God. This devotional will help you do just that. Erin humbly blends wisdom gained from her daughter's heaven going, with a strong grasp of the Biblical narrative, to remind and move you toward the simple, profound joys of walking with Christ through grief and heartache. If you know sorrow and want to reclaim hope, this devotional is for you."
Jennie Parks, *Executive Director of Hope Mommies.*

"Women grieving the loss of a child desperately need to know they aren't alone. But they also need to know God hasn't forgotten them. Erin has given us a book that does both. She takes us to the word and to the throne of grace in worship and in prayer. And there we find hope and healing in our time of need. I wish I had this book when I walked through our own losses. This is a gift to women walking through the deep valley of grief."
Courtney Reissig, author of *Teach Me to Feel: Worshiping Through the Psalms in Every Season of Life.*

2

"In a broken world, loss haunts us. To live resilient, we need the indomitable grace and durable hope grounded in the gospel and celebrated in this thoughtful devotional. If this is a season of grief, let the reflections and meditations within *Bright Hope* become a guide for your soul. Let the days be your fresh start. You won't regret it."

> **Dr. Dave Harvey,** *President of Great Commission Collective, author of When Sinners Say I Do and I Still Do (RevDaveHarvey.com)*

"Sorrow, disappointment, and pain are such a common reality in this fallen world. It has been my experience as a pastor and counselor for many years that oftentimes people don't know how or where to take these struggles. Erin has put together a wonderfully practical but amazingly deep resource to help people draw their hearts into the goodness and healing beauties of Jesus Christ. I am grateful for how Erin has used her own testimony of God's healing grace through sorrow to point other people to the hope extended through Jesus. I will be using this resource in our counseling ministries to equip and encourage through soul care.

> **Lee Lewis,** *Pastor of Soul Care at Radiant Church Austin; serves in a directing role in Soul Care Consulting.*

Bright Hope

28 Daily Devotions for Grief in Light of the Gospel

Erin Cushman

For Blakelee
and her parents, who have invited me in
to behold anew the mercies of God in the depths of loss.

CONTENTS

INTRODUCTION

In the afternoon of October 18, 2010, my world shifted. My firstborn, Gwendolyn Hope Cushman, was born after twenty-three hours of labor and an emergency cesarean. She was born without a heartbeat, but the doctor was able to revive her. For thirty-six hours my heart vacillated between extreme grief and a wild hope, as I followed the blips of her monitor and received updates from the doctors. It became clear that my beautiful firstborn's body was failing, and that death was inevitable. Our Gwendolyn went home to Heaven on October 20, 2010.

In the ten years I have had to adjust to life after loss, I have found grief to be a laborious journey. At the beginning, simply getting out of bed felt like a feat worthy of applause. There have been seasons of slogging along doing whatever I can to keep my head up and moving forward with routines, work, family, and faith. There have been seasons of stillness as the Lord worked through His word, His Spirit, and His people to bind up my broken heart. And there have been many seasons of joy as I grew in my understanding of what He accomplished for me and Gwendolyn when He died and rose again, conquering that great enemy, Death.

The burden of grief was made bearable — or heavier and harder — by two things: the internal dialogue I recited and the company I kept. No person speaks to us as often as we do to ourselves, and what we set our minds on has a profound impact on our heart. I soon realized that unless I had something good, true, secure, and hopeful to consciously focus on, my thoughts and emotions would quickly spiral down, landing in despair, hopelessness, anger, and isolation.

I also found that I needed good company for the journey. I needed to lean hard on the friendship of other Christians and the examples set by saints of old. We are designed for community. I needed people alongside me, yes, but I also needed to know that the pathway of grief has been trod upon before, and those pilgrims made it to the other side. Charles Spurgeon, a 19th century pastor, said it this way: "The comfort obtained by others may often prove helpful to another, just as wells would be used by those who come after. We read some good book full of consolation. Ah! We think our brother has been there before us and dug this well for us as well as for himself. Travelers have been delighted to see the footprints of a man on a barren shore, and we love to see the waymarks of pilgrims while passing through the vale of tears."[1] Reading through the narratives (both Biblical and biographical) of believers who have endured much, yet still remained hopeful and steadfast, buoyed my faith.

I also found great encouragement in my grief through music. Songs and poetry have been the medium of the soul since creation – Adam's first recorded words in Genesis 2:23 were a poem regarding Eve! Music can remind us of truth, fill us with comfort and hope, and melody has a beautiful habit of being retained in memory oftentimes better than reading literature. Great hymns have been sung for generations, such as It is Well or Rock of Ages, because they remain timeless in their truth, beauty, and application. At a retreat for grieving moms, singer/songwriter Sandra McCracken said that "We sing our faith forward."[2] As we sing words full of God's truth, we pull our struggling hearts along the way of faith and tether them to God's steadfast love.

My hope for this devotional is that it will help and encourage you to redirect your heart and mind to meditate on what is good, find company in the "cloud of witnesses"[3] who have gone before us through their poetry and song, and ultimately lead you to the comfort and hope found solely in the person of Jesus Christ.

I am praying that through this small offering from a fellow pilgrim, you will come to a deeper understanding of these words from 2 Thessalonians 2:16-17:

"Now may our Lord Jesus Christ himself, and God our Father, who loved us and gave us eternal comfort and good hope through grace, comfort your hearts and establish them in every good work and word."

Because He lives, I hope,

Erin Cushman

HOW TO USE THIS DEVOTIONAL

WEEKLY THEME

The book is in four sections meant to be read over 28 days. Each section, or week, is centered around a theme to help prompt your heart and mind to engage with the Lord. You can take it a day at a time or read all the week's devotionals at once.

The themes themselves are consistent throughout Scripture, and I hope that what is written here will launch you into seeing these truths throughout the entire Bible. Scripture quotes and references have been annotated, and you can find the verses at the notes section at the end of the book. With the conclusion of each day are Scripture references for further study. A devotional never replaces the Word of God and should always be measured by it, but one can serve as a starting place to behold anew the beauty of Jesus from an alternate view.

MEDITATING UPON A HYMN

Hymns are poetry, and poetry is meant to be savored. Before the Bible was easily accessible and literacy was common, hymns were taught and sung to communicate the truths of the Bible and cause the singer to think deeply on the meaning and application therein.

Day 6 of each week includes a hymn for meditation. The four hymns included were written by various authors from the 18th-20th centuries. Read them aloud, listen to them, sing them, research them and the story behind the words – give attention to the lyrics that have long sustained many a believer with their encouragement.

JOURNAL

2 Corinthians 9:6 encourages us, "The point is this: whoever sows sparingly will also reap sparingly, and whoever sows bountifully will also reap bountifully." A direct correlation to what you'll reap from this devotional is based upon what you sow in your heart and mind from it. Day 7 of each section has summary questions and journaling space for you to use as you reflect on what you learned throughout that week's devotions.

MUSIC

As a devotional seeking to highlight the blessing of music to encourage the soul, there are curated playlists for each week of the study. Using the music platforms of Spotify and Apple Music, you can find these playlists to encourage you as you read this devotional. You can find the playlists at hopemommies.org/brighthope

Here
bring your

wounded

hearts,

here tell your
anguish

WEEK 1

Come

*Come to me, all who labor and are heavy laden, and I will give you
rest. Take my yoke upon you, and learn from me, for I am gentle
and lowly in heart, and you will find rest for your souls.
For my yoke is easy, and my burden is light.*
- Matthew 11:28-30 -

In the gospel of Matthew, we find a breath of fresh air as Jesus
offers an invitation with no expiration date. It has no criteria,
no expectations — His call is simply an acknowledgement that
life is often full of weariness and heavy burdens, and that
reprieve and rest are found in Him.

Over the next several pages we will take time to come
before the Lord, learning what it means to do so desperately,
humbly, daily, persistently, and in faith.

Come: DESPERATELY

Come quickly, LORD, and answer me,
for my depression deepens.
- Psalm 143:7a NLT -

Grief makes us desperate. Desperate for answers, for time to reverse itself; desperate for one last moment with our beloved.

Impatient to escape from the constant pain; frantic for understanding; desperate for good. Grief is all consuming, taking over the heart, mind, and body. It feels inescapable, and depression deepens.

David, the psalmist that penned Psalm 143, understood that all-consuming desperation. He was in dire circumstances, overwhelmed by fear and in very real danger. In that intensity of emotion, he brought his whole heart before the Lord. He was in distressing circumstances yes, but ran to the God who rescues. He pleaded that God would show him His perfect, unfailing love.[4] That is what David needed most. It is what a grieving heart needs most.

His appeal to God shows us two things about genuine faith: it knows *Who can help*, and it knows *what He can do*. David threw all of his hope for help on the Lord. He came to God with a bold appeal, over and over, desperate to have God intervene and answer him. David didn't spend his time problem solving for himself, taking endless counsel with others, or ignoring the pain until it passed. David was not waiting on the passing of time to mitigate the pain.

David's first response was a heartfelt appeal to the God of steadfast love to act.

REFLECTION QUESTIONS

Read Psalm 143. Say aloud all the ways that David expects or asks God to act.

What are you hoping for or expecting from God in your own circumstances?

For further study: Psalm 13, Psalm 69

Come: HUMBLY

But this is the one to whom I will look:
he who is humble and contrite in spirit
and trembles at my word.
- Isaiah 66:2b -

Do you want God's attention? I do. I want His eye on me,[5] listening closely to me when I pray.[6] I want His heart to be tender regarding my circumstances and needs.[7] I want Him to actively be at work in my life for my good.[8]

Isaiah 66:2 tells us where God's attention rests. God bends low to care for those who are humble, contrite in spirit, and trembling at His word. To humble ourselves before God means we recognize that He is Creator and that we are not. He is all knowing; we are not. He is perfect; we are not. Humility is having a right perspective of your position before a Holy God. To be contrite in spirit, then, is to recognize our sin nature and inability to save ourselves. It is a soul-felt humility and sorrow for sinning against a Holy God. To tremble at His word is having a reverence and respect for the significance and weight of His words.

Consider for a moment how we respond when we are sick or have an emergency. We call 9-1-1 or urgently seek medical care and advice. We take seriously the information given to us by medical professionals based on their status, education, and authority. We recognize that they most likely know what they are talking about, and we give reverence and respect to their

23

position, valuing what they say to us. We follow their recommendations for our health and well-being.

If we respond this way to our fellow man because of their knowledge and experience, how much more should we respect and tremble at the words of the God of creation? It is in Him that "we live and move and have our being."[9] Pause and behold the Lord, who has greater knowledge, skill, and compassion than any earthly counselor.

REFLECTION QUESTIONS

Read Isaiah 57:15, James 4:6, and 1 Peter 5:5-7. What do these verses have in common about the relationship between mankind's actions and God's actions?

What is your heart posture before the Lord? Take a few moments to prayerfully humble yourself before the Lord and ask for His help.

For further study: Philippians 2

DAY 3

Come: DAILY

Behold, I am about to rain bread from heaven for you, and the
people shall go out and gather a day's portion every day, that I may
test them, whether they will walk in my law or not.
- Exodus 16:4 -

On the days when grief felt so heavy, just making it until bedtime was my sole focus. When my mind would jump forward and think of days upon days of feeling the same way, anxiety and despair would quickly overwhelm me.

God understands the depth and range of human emotions. He also understands our limited capacity for managing them. In Psalm 103:14 it says, "For he knows our frame; he remembers that we are dust." God wisely created beings in His image but designed them to be needy. Even before Adam and Eve ate the fruit and brought sin into the world, they were dependent on God every moment of the day.

In Exodus we learn about God working astounding miracles as He led the Israelites out of Egypt, parting the Red Sea and moving among them in a cloud of fire to protect and lead them. When they came to the wilderness, the people despaired and complained. I am sure they felt anxious and worried about their families. They needed food and water and also wanted some normality.

But God designed His creatures to be dependent on Him for their needs, to look to their Creator for their normal. He designed manna for Israel – an unusual substance for making bread – to rain down on them every day. Six days a week they went out to gather it. If they gathered too much and tried to hoard it over until the next day, it would rot. But on the sixth day, they could gather double and it would not rot so they could worship and rest on the Sabbath. God was providing just what they needed on a moment-by-moment basis.

God used their desert wanderings to test and reveal the condition of their hearts. Would they depend on Him and trust His daily care for them? Or would they try to be self-sustaining, storing up what they needed on their own? Would they reject His provision altogether and refuse to go out and gather?

It was not as if God was conducting a test about the posture of their heart because He was unsure of the answer. God is intimately aware of every thought and feeling of every human, in every place,[10] and knows the end from the beginning.[11] His test was for their benefit, that they would glimpse the condition of their own hearts, turn in repentance, and trust His provision.

REFLECTION QUESTIONS

What needs are pressing on you right now?

How can you come to God for your daily needs?

For further study: Isaiah 55

DAY 4

Come: PERSISTENTLY

And he told them a parable to the effect
that they ought always to pray and not lose heart.
- Luke 18:1 -

Have you ever found it hard to pray?

After our daughter died, I struggled to pray – to believe that it mattered if I did. The disciples and the crowds in Jesus' day did too, which is why in Luke 18 Jesus tells an incredible parable about a widow seeking justice from an arrogant, indolent judge. In the parable, the woman comes day after day without giving up, pleading her cause before an uncaring man. Eventually the judge is so exasperated by her coming that he gives her what she wants and acts on her behalf. Then Jesus draws the parallel: if an unrighteous, imperfect, selfish judge eventually yields to the supplications of the widow, how much more will God the Father eagerly respond to the cries of His children?

It is the character of God that gives us confidence to not lose heart when we pray. We are not approaching an unfeeling, self-driven human with our needs and desires. We are coming before a holy, loving, compassionate, powerful God. A Father God, who has adopted individuals into His family at great cost.[12] A Holy God, who is faultless and just at every moment.[13] A perfect God, who is never lazy or unrighteous. A gentle God, who places immense value on widows and orphans[14] and those who are downcast or forgotten. God draws near to those who are brokenhearted and contrite,[15] and He does not respond with exasperation as the unrighteous judge did. He does not delay but answers speedily.[16]

When we come before God, prayer acts as a mirror to our hearts. Are we distracted, mumbling practiced phrases? Are we haphazard in our approach, praying only when we remember to? Is prayer a priority or merely an accessory to our life? God has created the pathways of prayer for us so we can be in relationship with Him. And God uses prayer to refine us, drilling down further and further into the motivation and desires that prompt our dialogue. What is it that we are truly asking for? What is the deepest longing we have? Are we bringing all of ourselves before the Lord, or are we holding back in fear or doubt? Do we come persistently and expectantly, or do we approach Him with timidity and doubt?

REFLECTION QUESTIONS

What is your attitude toward and practice of prayer?

What is the deepest request and desire of your heart in this time? Take some moments to bring that desire before the Lord.

For further study: Psalm 34

DAY 5

Come: IN FAITH

And without faith it is impossible to please him, for whoever
would draw near to God must believe that he exists and that he
rewards those who seek him.
- Hebrews 11:6 -

Sometimes we really overcomplicate faith. Hebrews 11 tells us the two simple truths that will take us into a deeper and richer faith:

1) God exists, and
2) He rewards those who seek Him.

God exists. Not multiple gods but One God,[17] eternally existing, never created;[18] dwelling in three Persons;[19] Creator of the universe,[20] holding all things together; perfect in His power,[21] love,[22] faithfulness, and justice;[23] revealing Himself to mankind through His created world,[24] His written word,[25] and His Son, Jesus.[26] God exists.

His reward for those who seek after and draw near to Him is more incredible than we could every fully grasp. It is not at all what our culture preaches. A physical, tangible reward (like fame or health or riches) would eventually fade; those have a dangerous tendency to steal our affections away from Him. The reward of God is actually Himself.[27] It is His salvation from sin and eternal suffering apart from Him.[28] It is His continual presence in our every circumstance.[29] It is His Spirit at work in us producing things like love, patience, joy, faithfulness, self-control, and peace.[30] He gives us hope of a future that is perfect and complete.[31] Whether or not we are always aware of it, God Himself is the longing of our heart.

REFLECTION QUESTIONS

Read Jeremiah 29:13 and Romans 10:9-17. What do these verses teach you about how to seek God in faith?

What do you think God is trying to teach you in your current circumstances?

For further study: Ephesians 2

DAY 6

Meditate:

COME, YE DISCONSOLATE

Come, ye disconsolate, where'er ye languish;
Come to the mercy-seat, fervently kneel;
Here bring your wounded hearts, here tell your anguish;
Earth has no sorrow that heav'n cannot heal.

Joy of the desolate, light of the straying,
Hope of the penitent, fadeless and pure,
Here speaks the Comforter, tenderly saying,
"Earth has no sorrow that heav'n cannot cure."

Here see the bread of life; see waters flowing
Forth from the throne of God, pure from above;
Come to the feast of love; come, ever knowing
Earth has its sorrow, but heav'n can remove.

Words by Thomas Moore (1816) and Thomas Hastings (1832).

DAY 7

Journal: WEEK IN REVIEW

Look back over the devotions from this week. Which was most significant to you?

What aspect of coming before the Lord do you find easy to do? What do you find difficult?

What line(s) from the hymn did you find meaningful?

Write out one verse or verses of Scripture that impacted you this week.

Heart of my own heart, whatever befall, *still be my vision*, O Ruler of all

WEEK 2

Behold

Say to those who have an anxious heart,
"Be strong; fear not! Behold, your God will come
with vengeance, with the recompense of God.
He will come and save you."
- Isaiah 35:4 -

The word "Behold" is meant to make us pause. It is often used in Scripture, and it is meant to cause us to stop and pay attention to what is about to be communicated. The connotation has much to do with quieting people in the presence of someone or some event of importance.[32]

When we hush our busy minds, steady our anxious hearts, and quietly behold the person of God through His word, transformation begins. We become what we behold. Throughout the next several days, we will take time to stop and consider a few characteristics of God. Let's quiet down the clamor of our own thoughts, step away from the ordinary business of our lives, and behold Him: His compassion, provision, sovereignty, mercy and grace, and His indwelling Spirit.

Behold: HIS COMPASSION

And when the Lord saw her, he had compassion on her
and said to her, "Do not weep."
- Luke 7:13 -

If you need a proof text on the compassion of Jesus for physical and emotional distresses during his earthly ministry, look no further than Luke 7. In that chapter you will meet a man of position and power of a different race and religion; a destitute and grieving mother; a devout disciple that was struggling with deep doubt; and a desperate woman that had been shunned all her life. And in each interaction with those individuals that range across the spectrum of reputation, status, and wealth we see Christ demonstrating His great compassion and empathy for their circumstances.

For the prominent centurion who humbly knew his own place before God, Jesus commended his faith and healed a beloved servant. For the lonely widow, He interrupted the funeral procession to raise her son from the dead and restore hope and joy. For John the Baptist, who had spent his whole life preparing the way for the Messiah and declared Jesus to be the Lamb of God, Jesus assured him that his faith was not in vain. For the penitent woman who knew her only hope of wholeness and purity would be found in Jesus, whose feet she wept over and washed with her tears, he pardoned her sin and gave her peace.

Jesus didn't discriminate based on status, need, or righteousness. He saw and heard their needs, both visible (the dying servant and dead son) and invisible (overwhelming doubt and crippling shame) and walked into their pain to alleviate it. And because Jesus is the same yesterday, today, and forever, He is able and willing to step into *your* pain and meet *your* needs as well.

REFLECTION QUESTIONS

Read Luke 7. Which character do you relate to right now, and why?

Read Romans 8:31-39. What from these verses comforts you?

For further study: Isaiah 53

DAY 2

Behold: HIS PROVISION

Know that the LORD, he is God!
It is he who made us, and we are his;
we are his people, and the sheep of his pasture.
- Psalm 100:3 -

Have you ever paused to consider the repeated imagery of sheep in the Bible? The nation of Israel is constantly likened to sheep. God declares that the leaders of Israel have been poor caretakers of the flock, and He will prove Himself to be the greater Shepherd.[33] The psalms are full of flocks and lambs. Jesus tells us that He is the good Shepherd, and His sheep know Him well.[34] The church is called "the flock" and pastors and elders are called to shepherd the flock with wisdom, so that when the Chief Shepherd appears, they may receive a blessing.[35] Jesus is the Lamb that was slain, taking away the sins of the world.[36]

Have you also considered the *value* of sheep? Sheep were a precious commodity in the early centuries and were the livelihood of many. A sheep produces wool, keeping its owners clothed and warm. Sheepskin was also made into clothing. For special occasions, their milk and meat provided a feast. For worship sacrifices, sheep were the typical offering. It was a lamb's blood that was used to mark the doorway during Passover. Sheep were often the bride-price paid to the bride's family upon marriage. Sheep were highly valued.

It follows then, that skillful tending of the sheep was of great importance. They were not carelessly bandied about.

Sheep needed care, green pasture, clean water, and protection from predators. They could not do any of that themselves, but were wholly dependent on the care of their shepherd.

When David spoke of being led by the great Shepherd in Psalm 23, he saw himself as being cared for tenderly and constantly. He looked expectantly to the Shepherd to provide. He found rest when the Shepherd was near. He was not anxious, because he knew Who was responsible for his needs. All that he needed was found in the provision of the One who led him.

When Jesus called Himself the great Shepherd in John 10, he said that His sheep "hear His voice, and He calls His own sheep by name and leads them out." Jesus intimately knows those who are His. He knows your name. He knows your individual needs. He will lead you in the way that is good for you.

REFLECTION QUESTIONS

Are there any areas of provision that you are anxious about?

What do you find comforting about being a sheep in God's care?

For further study: John 10

Behold: HIS SOVEREIGNTY

If I take the wings of the morning
and dwell in the uttermost parts of the sea,
even there your hand shall lead me,
and your right hand shall hold me.
- Psalm 139:9-10 -

At this very moment, you are being sustained by God.

Psalm 139 is a sweeping panorama of the sovereignty of God. Take a moment to read through its entirety. At once you get the impression that God is everywhere, knows everything, is incredibly powerful, and is deeply personal. Let's pause to consider the glory of each of these truths.

In David's day, the surrounding nations worshipped multiple deities. These 'gods' were specific to various people groups,[37] were fickle and unreliable, constrained in knowledge and power.[38] But the true and only God is limitless. Nothing in all creation is outside of His jurisdiction. It is impossible to hide from the presence of God, even if you should wish it. He is not bound by any human constructs.

He is also limitless in His knowledge. He knows what will be said before it is said. He is infinite in His wisdom and thoughts, which David describes as being "more than the sand."

The LORD God is absolutely powerful. He creates every life, determining down to the minute how long that life will be sustained on Earth. His hand is at work in every moment. His hand is currently upholding you and all that you see.[39]

And most incredible and delightful of all, God is deeply personal. He is not like a lifeguard on the beach, surveying the general crowd and responding only to distress calls or rabble-rousers. When the Lord says in Psalm 32:8, "I will counsel you with my eye upon you," He is illuminating an intimate relationship. The Creator of the universe *knows* you.

David understands how impossible all of these qualities of God are to hold in one hand. Especially from a grieving perspective, the sovereign care of God is difficult to wrap our minds around. But we must agree with David as he exclaims, "How precious to me are your thoughts, O God! How vast is the sum of them!" He is trusting that what he doesn't understand still falls under the umbrella of God's good and omniscient personal care of his life.

REFLECTION QUESTIONS

What verses in Psalm 139 capture your attention?

How is God sovereignly caring for you today?

Further study: Matthew 6:25-34

Behold: HIS MERCY

Good and upright is the LORD;
therefore he instructs sinners in the way.
- Psalm 25:8 -

What does it mean for God to be good and upright?

Often we define those qualities by what they are *not* – not bad, wicked, unkind, immoral, wrong, duplicitous, snarky, scheming, or evil. Those are the qualities inherited by Adam's children,[40] but they are never true of God. God, of course, would be completely justified if the verse from Psalm 25 read, "Good and upright is the LORD; therefore He smites all sinners and punishes them forever." But that is *not* what it says! "*Good* and *upright* is the LORD; *therefore* he *instructs* sinners in the way.*" It is His goodness and His love for righteousness coupled with His compassionate love for sinners that takes the progression from deserved punishment for sinners to incredible gifts of grace.

In place of His justified wrath, He gives pardon to those who receive it.[41] In place of ignorance and a heart that is bent toward sin, He gives a new heart that will love what is good and walk in the right way.[42] In place of an eternity separated from Him, He gives us a perfect substitute for our sin and grants eternal life to those who believe in His Son, Jesus.[43]

Not only do we escape His wrath – that's His mercy at work -- we also receive boundless gifts of grace. It is nothing but the compassion of the Lord towards us that grants us such riches. Whatever circumstance you are facing, you can be assured that

God's eye is on you, His ear is attentive to your cry, and He is
leading you in the right way.[44]

REFLECTION QUESTIONS

*God offers His mercy and grace to all, but it requires repentance and
faith to receive it. Read Romans 10:9-17. What do those verses say
regarding our response to God's mercy?*

What decision have you made regarding Christ's offer?

For further study: Romans 5

DAY 5

$\mathcal{B}$ehold: HIS SPIRIT IN US

And I will ask the Father, and he will give you another Helper, to be
with you forever, even the Spirit of truth, whom the world cannot
receive, because it neither sees him nor knows him. You know him,
for he dwells with you and will be in you.
- John 14:16-17 -

Jesus knew that it would be better for His people to have the Spirit of God living in them rather than He, Jesus, living beside them. It was the will of God for Jesus to go and prepare a place for us[45] and to intercede for us.[46] He then sent His own Spirit to be a counselor, advocate, encourager, and helper to us who believe.[47]

Having the indwelling Spirit is not as if we lose our personality and begin acting like a robot that was hacked by an outside source. We were created to be a representation of God – a physical likeness of an invisible God in the way that we reflect His goodness, mercy, love, justice, righteousness, holiness, etc. Sin ruined the image-bearers, distorting the reflection. But when we are filled with His Spirit, the transformative heart work begins as we are, by degrees, molded into the fullest version of ourselves.[48]

Do you feel alone? If you are the Lord's, then you are never alone, for He promised never to leave or forsake you.[49] Do you need wisdom? The Spirit of wisdom and revelation dwells in you.[50] Do you feel anxious or hopeless? The God of hope, joy and peace has given you Himself so that you may abound in hope and always be at peace.[51]

When you pause to consider and behold that a perfect and Holy God would choose to dwell in and with mankind, it is knowledge too wonderful for us to fully comprehend. It is not for us to know all the details of *how* God can give us a new heart and spirit, as He promises in Ezekiel 36. But it is enough for us to rest in the knowledge that He does.

REFLECTION QUESTIONS

Read John 14:1-18. Describe why Jesus said that it was better for the Holy Spirit to come.

How have you seen the Spirit work in you and around you?

For further study: Ephesians 4

DAY 6

Meditate:

BE THOU MY VISION

Be thou my vision, O Lord of my heart;
Naught be all else to me, save that thou art–
Thou my best thought by day or by night,
Waking or sleeping, thy presence my light.

Be thou my wisdom, and thou my true word;
I ever with thee and thou with me, Lord;
Thou my great Father, I thy true son;
Thou in me dwelling, and I with thee one.

Be thou my battle shield, sword for my fight;
Be thou my dignity, thou my delight,
Thou my soul's shelter, thou my high tow'r:
Raise thou me heav'n-ward, O Pow'r of my pow'r.

Riches I heed not, nor man's empty praise,
Thou mine inheritance, now and always:
Thou and thou only, first in my heart,
High King of heaven, my treasure thou art.

High King of heaven, my victory won,
May I reach heaven's joys, O bright heav'n's Sun!
Heart of my own heart, whatever befall,
Still be my vision, O Ruler of all.

Text from 8th century Irish hymn; translated by Mary E. Byrne (1905).

DAY 7

Journal: WEEK IN REVIEW

Look back over the devotions from this week. Which was most significant to you?

What aspect of beholding the Lord do you find easy to do? What do you find difficult?

What line(s) from the hymn did you find meaningful?

Write out one verse or verses of Scripture that impacted you this week.

Dear
Refuge of My

Weary

Soul

WEEK 3

Find

Every good gift and every perfect gift is from above, coming down from the Father of lights with whom there is no variation or shadow due to change.
- James 1:17 -

God is a generous giver. He is not begrudging or regretful when His gifts are neglected or unappreciated. He doesn't take them back. It is His nature to be lavish and generous, overflowing the banks of the souls of mankind with His grace. It is because He is unchanging that we can find an abundance of comfort and hope. If He is the same yesterday, today, and forever (and He is),[52] then what He supplied to Abraham and Sarah, to the nation of Israel, to the prophets, to Mary Magdalene, to Paul, and to the early Church He can and will also do for us. This is not to say that the gifts will be exactly the same, but the nature of the Giver is reliable and His understanding of our needs is perfect. He will supply for them completely through Jesus Christ.

This week we will look at what He promises we will find when we ask, seek and knock.[53] Refuge, strength, comfort, joy, and hope are yours as you seek after the God who never changes.

Find : REFUGE

Be merciful to me, O God, be merciful to me, for in you my soul takes refuge; in the shadow of your wings I will take refuge, till the storms of destruction pass by. I cry out to God Most High, to God who fulfills his purpose for me.

- Psalm 57:1-2 -

Do you have days when you long to hit the "pause" button and step away from whatever is overwhelming you at the moment? On the days when it all feels too much, God's promise of refuge is a sweet comfort. Whether my "too much" is from grief, stress, exhaustion, a long to-do list, anxiety, or relationships that are strained and weighty, the idea of taking cover under the wings of the Lord has been what I have needed — more than a relaxing conversation with a friend, more than delegating tasks, more than chocolate or a glass of wine or a weekend away. God's rest is more filling to our souls than any of His created gifts.

God created us to be needy. Psalm 103:14 says that God "knows our frame; he remembers that we are dust." He knows how quickly we change from day to day in our emotions and thoughts. But *He* is unchanging and always running on full. He never grows tired or weary, and He extends His own fullness to us when we seek and find our refuge in Him.

Are you feeling overwhelmed? Ask Him, and He will shoulder your burden. Are you anxious? Talk to Him; He will take on your worries. Are you exhausted? Come to Him; He will revive you. Are you insecure and fearful? Cry out to Him; He will remind you of who you are in Him.

If you are longing to escape from whatever is too much, run to Him in prayer and seek Him through His word. He promises shelter from storms and comfort under His wings when you cry out to Him.[54]

REFLECTION QUESTIONS

What is overwhelming you today?

Say a prayer of dependence, asking the Lord to be your refuge.

Further study: Psalm 18, Psalm 62

Find : STRENGTH

My flesh and my heart may fail,
but God is the strength of my heart and my portion forever.
- Psalm 73:26 -

God designed humankind to have bodies. Pause and consider the implications of that. He intended for men and women to have physical properties, needs, abilities, and to function in specific and limited capacities. When God created Adam and had all the animals participate in the "Name Me Parade" in Genesis, He did it intentionally to show Adam his otherness. [55] Adam was different than all the animals, and he needed a counterpart.

Enter Woman: her femininity and his masculinity were similar, yet distinct — equal in value, different in function. And their bodies had constraints. They required food and water, sleep and shelter. There was a limit to their physicality and strength, even in Eden.

The physical needs of humanity are quite obvious and yet easily forgotten until they are threatened. Our limits are realized in weakness: when hunger claws an empty belly; when physical ailment or surgery impede our movement; when we cannot force our bodies to stay awake a moment longer. We have many needs beyond our ability. Continuing on after grief is a need beyond our ability. It requires *capability* and *perseverance* of body and heart, a strength beyond our reach.

Enter the Lord: "The Creator of the ends of the earth. He does not faint or grow weary; his understanding is unsearchable. He gives power to the faint, and to him who has no might he increases strength," (Isaiah 40:28b-29).

The Lord understands the limits of our heart, mind, and body better than we do. He knows that on our best day, we don't have what it takes to endure. He willingly and joyfully steps in to give us His strength, His heart, His perseverance. As the hymn *Great is Thy Faithfulness* words it, He gives "strength for today and bright hope for tomorrow." If you find yourself straining toward the end of your ability today, I encourage you to simply stop where you are and ask the Lord to be the strength of your heart and to be your portion for the day.

REFLECTION QUESTIONS

Describe a time when you felt utterly spent, at the end of your strength. What revived you?

What do you need God's strength for today?

For further study: Psalm 91

DAY 3

Find : COMFORT

Blessed be the God and Father of our Lord Jesus Christ,
the Father of mercies and God of all comfort, who comforts us
in all our affliction, so that we may be able to comfort those who are
in any affliction, with the comfort with which we ourselves are
comforted by God. For as we share abundantly in Christ's
sufferings, so through Christ we share abundantly
in comfort too.
- 2 Corinthians 1:3-5 -

Read through the verses above, and observe what it tells us about the character and actions of God:

He is worthy of being blessed.

He is the God and Father of Jesus Christ.

He is a Father of mercies.

He is the God of all comfort.

He comforts us in all our affliction.

What a precious promise! He is God of *all* comfort – not partial, not only for an hour or a day. His comfort is not medication that wears off. Comprehensive comfort is found in God alone. And He comforts us in *all* our affliction. Sickness, suffering, hardship, complaint, pain, conflict – *all* of what troubles us is welcome under His banner of comfort.

A powerful but unstated assumption is present in these verses. It is expected that as children of God we would seek to be comforted by God. However, even though comfort is part of His character and what He offers us, we don't automatically take hold of it. God continually calls and offers salvation, hope, wisdom, and forgiveness, yet so often those gifts are rejected. Why? Because being comforted by God requires vulnerability.

Now, transparency and vulnerability are not synonymous. Transparency says, "Here are all my troubles." Vulnerability says, "Here are all my troubles… will you help me?"[56] Being vulnerable before God is a willingness to come and express how greatly we are hurting and how much we need His rescue. Comfort — reassurance, relief, cheer, encouragement — is freely offered to you. Choose today to expose your need to God and ask Him to give you what He promises: an abundance of comfort so overflowing and complete that when the time comes, you can extend that comfort toward others in any affliction or trouble they face.

REFLECTION QUESTIONS

Why do we find it difficult to be vulnerable before the Lord?

How has God used others to comfort you? How have you been able to comfort others?

For further study: 2 Corinthians 5

DAY 4

Find: JOY

Though the fig tree should not blossom,
nor fruit be on the vines,
the produce of the olive fail
and the fields yield no food,
the flock be cut off from the fold
and there be no herd in the stalls,
yet I will rejoice in the LORD;
I will take joy in the God of my salvation.
- Habakkuk 3:17-18 -

Habakkuk was a prophet during the decline of the Judean
kingdom. In his lifetime, he had seen great prosperity and
security and then had that security stripped away as an army
invaded their land, bringing chaos, death, and destruction.
The book of Habakkuk is short but full of a man's earnest
entreaties to understand how God could still be good and just
in the face of such tragedy.

Sound familiar? Take a few minutes to read through the
book (it's only three chapters!). Can you hear his questions?
Do they sound like yours? He's questioning the goodness of
God, the justice of God, the wisdom of God, the love of God. I
did the same when holding my daughter's dying body. As I
watched her gasp her last shuddering breath and the evidence
of death overtook her beloved features, I saw only emptiness
ahead of me. My doubts ran deep in the days and months that
followed.

Habakkuk's conclusion then in chapter three is remarkable.
Though emptiness was all he saw and knew, *yet even still*, He

chose to rejoice in the Lord. How is that possible? The answer is that he depended on the Lord to be his fullness, not on his circumstances. Everything around him *was* empty. But the LORD is the same as He always had been, and Habakkuk took time to catalogue God's faithfulness in years past. His ability to rejoice was not because His circumstances changed, but because his God was unchangingly loving, kind, faithful, and just. Because God is who He is, Habakkuk rejoiced in a salvation that was yet to come and rested in the promise of God's strength to be enough and God's power to lift him out of his trouble.[57]

REFLECTION QUESTIONS

What questions do you have for God right now?

Look back on God's actions throughout your life. Journal a few ways that God has demonstrated His faithfulness to you.

For further study: 2 Corinthians 4

DAY 5

Find: HOPE

My soul is bereft of peace; I have forgotten what happiness is;
so I say, 'My endurance has perished;
so has my hope from the Lord.'
- Lamentations 3:17-18 -

Lamentations 3 became a landing place for me in the days following Gwendolyn's death. It moans and weeps, expresses doubt and depression, faith and a fierce hope all in one chapter. The book of Lamentations was written during the siege of Jerusalem around 600BC[58]. It is a sweeping lament (thus the name) over the atrocities of sin that led them to being surrounded by enemies. It described what they experienced during that time and the hopelessness of their situation. When the author burst out in despair, he was being honest, not dramatic.

But through the fog of his grief and despondency, his mind cleared as he reminded himself of God's character when he wrote verses 21-25:

But this I call to mind, and therefore I have hope:
the steadfast love of the LORD never ceases;
his mercies never come to an end;
they are new every morning;
great is your faithfulness.
"The LORD is my portion," says my soul,
"therefore I will hope in him."
The Lord is good to those who wait for him,
to the soul who seeks him.

He was not looking ahead to a future of familial, political, physical, or financial security to ease his pain. His hope was not that one day their circumstances would change and that time would heal all their wounds. No, he looked back on God's covenant and drew all his hope and strength from God's faithful love in years past. I can imagine that his reflection went something like this:

"God made a covenant, a vow.[59] God never lies.[60] He said He will be faithful. He said He's steadfast and unshakeable in His love toward us.[61] He said He'll never leave us.[62] He said He can do the impossible.[63] He said He abounds in love and mercy.[64] He's gracious, giving us gifts we don't deserve. He's patient and kind when we are weak and doubtful.[65] He's full of wisdom[66] and truth.[67] He forgives us when we repent.[68] He does not treat us as our sins deserve.[69] He acts in ways we don't comprehend,[70] but that doesn't nullify His perfection and love. If He is all of that and beyond, and I am His... the result of all this must be that there is a hope for my future,[71] and I can wait on Him to make it right."

REFLECTION QUESTIONS

What resonates with you from Lamentations 3?

What is your hope?

For further study: 1 Corinthians 15

Meditate:

DEAR REFUGE
OF MY WEARY SOUL

Dear refuge of my weary soul,
On thee when sorrows rise;
On thee, when waves of trouble roll,
My fainting hope relies.
To thee I tell each rising grief,
For thou alone canst heal;
Thy word can bring a sweet relief,
For every pain I feel.

But oh! When gloomy doubts prevail
I fear to call thee mine;
The springs of comfort seem to fail
And all my hopes decline.
Yet gracious God, where shall I flee?
Thou art my only trust;
And still my soul would cleave to thee,
Though prostrate in the dust.

Hast thou not bid me seek thy face?
And shall I seek in vain?
And can the ear of sovereign grace
Be deaf when I complain?
No, still the ear of sovereign grace
Attends the mourner's prayer;
O may I ever find access,
To breathe my sorrows there.

Thy mercy-seat is open still;
Here let my soul retreat,
With humble hope attend thy will,
And wait beneath thy feet.

Words by Anne Steele (1760).

Journal: WEEK IN REVIEW

Look back over the devotions from this week. Which was most significant to you?

What is easy for you to find as you come to the Lord? What do you find more elusive or difficult?

What line(s) from the hymn did you find meaningful?

Write out one verse or verses of Scripture that impacted you this week.

Strength
for today,

bright

hope

for tomorrow.

Walk

If we live by the Spirit, let us also keep in step with the Spirit.
- Galatians 5:25 -

As I am sure you have heard or are coming to learn, grief is a process, not an event. While a crisis – one horrible moment – has brought you to the precipice of this journey, moving through grief is a progression, with no clear road map or "perfect" way forward.

What *is* certain is that if you are adopted into the Lord's family, you are not alone on the journey. Deuteronomy 31:8 says, "It is the LORD who goes before you. He will be with you; he will not leave you or forsake you. Do not fear or be dismayed." The Lord promised to light a way in the darkness, making paths where there were none.[72] He promised to go with us as our guide, and it is His presence going with us that makes all the difference, sustaining a weary pilgrim's soul.

This week we will look at five of God's promises that are rooted in His character that will transform and sustain us as we walk through grief. As we think about how to walk in peace, trust, forgiveness, gratitude, and grace, I am confident that we will find that His faithfulness keeps step with us at every moment.

DAY 1

Walk: IN TRUST

To you, O LORD, I lift up my soul.
O my God, in you I trust; let me not be put to shame;
let not my enemies exult over me.
Indeed, none who wait for you shall be put to shame.
- Psalm 25:1-3a -

How would you define or describe trust? A quick dictionary search will provide many synonyms for it: rely, count on, believe, depend, have confidence in... one of my favorites analogies for trust is expressed in the idiom, "having all your eggs in one basket."

Trust and its antonym, doubt, are intrinsic to who we are. Adam and Eve were created beings, inherently reliant and trusting upon God. Humanity is wired for dependency. But when the serpent whispered half-truths to Eve, he was sowing seeds of doubt that have grown a weedy harvest ever since. Doubt casts aspersions on the character of God. Doubt whispers that He is not good. Doubt preys upon unanswered questions and prayers.

James 1:6 says, "The one who doubts is like a wave of the sea, that is driven and tossed by the wind." In other words the one who lives with a distrustful, uncertain heart is unstable in all their ways. Who desires a reality like that? To be insecure and unsteady, always filled with apprehension and misgiving? Never fully surrendered, sure that some heartbreak or worse is just around the next corner? Choosing to trust – and then choosing again and again as doubts surface

– is the only way to conquer the unrest and hopelessness that doubt brings.

Praise God, for He is worthy of trust. He has a character that never changes, develops, or ages.[73] He is constant in His affections and purposes.[74] Whatever He does, He does well.[75] Unlike us, He remains steadfast at all times and new mercies arise for each need of the day.[76] He is the only safe 'basket' for all your 'eggs' to go into. He promises that those who trust in Him will never be ashamed.[77] There will never be cause to regret trusting Him fully; there will only be regret for the opposite.

REFLECTION QUESTIONS

What doubts or uncertainties are you facing?

Express a prayer of dependence on the Lord using different synonyms for trust. I trust you, Lord. I rely upon you. I depend on you to _____, etc.

Further study: James 1, Psalm 25

DAY 2

Walk: IN PEACE

You keep him in perfect peace whose mind is stayed on you,
because he trusts in you. Trust in the LORD forever,
for the LORD God is an everlasting rock.
- Isaiah 26:3-4 -

Ever since Adam and Eve doubted and disobeyed the Lord in Genesis 3, passing down that sin to all of humanity,[78] our natural inclination is to assume control and attempt to operate autonomously. When life squeezes us and we realize just how little control we actually have, our hearts and minds instantly spiral toward anxiety and panic. We clutch for power, passively or actively. The fear at the root of our scrambling can make us run in avoidance and shut down, or we try harder to maintain a façade of having it all together as we strive to "live our best life now".

Consider how our culture encourages us to respond. Stress management, therapies, techniques, practices… there are entire sections of bookstores dedicated to helping us reassert our control over circumstances, relationships, and our attitudes regarding them. The abundance of options gives some indication of how effective they are at completely relieving anxiety and producing peace!

But thanks be to God, there is a sure and steadfast way to find peace. It is found in following the Prince of Peace[79] wherever He may lead. Peace is on the other side of submitting all our cares and anxieties to Him, trusting Him to work for us.[80] There is peace in believing that His strength is sufficient

77

and can weather every storm.[81] God is a God of hope and fills us with peace,[82] promising a tranquility so strong that it protects and guards our hearts and minds.

Just as our emotions change from day to day, so too can our perception of peace. One difficult conversation, one social media post, one memory, one offhanded comment… the small and innocuous matters can easily throw off any peace or calm we had in a moment.

God is familiar with all our emotions – and all our burdens and anxieties. He knows when we are anxious and that He Himself is the only solution for peace amidst the chaos. He invites us to bring all of our cares, worries, thoughts, and fears to Him at every moment. He never shames us or shakes His head in annoyance. Instead, with a promise that His perfect peace will guard our hearts and minds, He invites us to come and rest in Him.[83]

REFLECTION QUESTIONS

What anxieties plague you today and threaten your peace?

Spend time in prayer, bringing your cares before the Lord.

For further study: Philippians 4

Walk: IN FORGIVENESS

Be kind to one another, tenderhearted,
forgiving one another, as God in Christ forgave you.
- Ephesians 4:32 -

I never knew how bruised and tender a heart could be until I grieved our daughter's death. And though I didn't have exterior marks that made my brokenness visible, some days I wished for that – if only so that others could understand how fragile I felt and why I might not behave in a way that is socially acceptable.

And like bruises that sting when lightly brushed against, I found my feelings easily hurt by what was said or unsaid, done or undone by others. I didn't know how to engage with people. I often walked away disappointed or feeling slightly wounded by the encounter.

Those emotions may be understandable, but they will influence us to act in one way or another. Biblical counselor Dr. Bob Kellemen wrote this about feelings: "The root of the word *emotion* is *motere*, from the Latin verb 'to move,' plus the prefix 'e' meaning 'to move away.' This suggests that a tendency to act is implicit in every emotion. All emotions are, in essence, inclinations to act and react. This means that *God designed our emotions to put us in motion.*"[84]

If left unchecked and unyielded to the Lord a grieving heart often moves toward unforgiveness and bitterness, especially in relationship to others. Emotions are good – we serve an emotional God. He rejoices,[85] grieves,[86] feels indignant,[87] and laughs.[88] We bear the image of an emotional God. But what should we do when we are filled with the hard emotions of offense, fear, loneliness, or sadness? Here is what the Word of God counsels when faced with such heaviness:

Pour out your heart to God.[89]

Cry out to Him.[90]

Find refuge and rest in Him.[91]

Seek the Lord when you're feeling afraid.[92]

Throw all of your anxiety on His shoulders.[93]

Rejoice in His perfect love that never fails.[94]

Consider Jesus, who faithfully endured hardship with joy.[95]

Forgive just as freely and completely as He forgave you.[96]

Do all that you can to live in peace with others.[97]

In Hebrews 12:14-15 the author exhorts the readers to be vigilant to pursue peaceful relationships: "Strive for peace with everyone, and for the holiness without which no one will see the Lord. See to it that no one fails to obtain the grace of God; that no 'root of bitterness' springs up and causes trouble." It takes willingness and humility to pursue healthy relationships: willingness to be vulnerable and humility to see where you may have been the one to cause offense. It takes grace – giving unmerited love, favor, and forgiveness – to cultivate that which is good, healthy, and growing. Otherwise, the author warns, a root of bitterness will spring up causing trouble and heartache, not just in the relationship, but in *you*. God uses those around us to help keep our hearts tender; He cannot heal a hardened, unforgiving, bitter heart[98].

Learning to reengage with others after grief is challenging but not impossible. As we take steps of obedience and pursue Christ-exalting relationships with those around us, we can be confident God is at work, smoothing out the hardened edges of our hearts and making us more like Himself.

REFLECTION QUESTIONS

What situations or relationships have caused hurt since your loss?

From the list above, how do you think God wants you to respond?

For further study: Romans 12, Matthew 18

DAY 4

Walk: IN GRATITUDE

Give thanks in all circumstances;
for this is the will of God in Christ Jesus for you.
- 1 Thessalonians 5:18 -

Praise, rejoicing, thankfulness, gratitude—those words are commonplace in our worship music, our prayers, and in the Word. They roll easily off the tongue when we are happy and life feels good. But what about when your heart is so broken you feel physically pained? When you can't see the road in front of you for the tears coursing down your face?

In Hebrews 13 we are called to continually give God a "sacrifice of praise".[99] Sacrifices are not easy or happenstance. They require intentionality and are costly to us.[100] To praise the Lord when you don't understand what He may be doing necessitates a profound trust in His goodness and absolute dependence on His love to carry you along in the darkness.

Our thanksgiving is prompted and undergirded by the gospel. When we glimpse the goodness of God, the travesty of our sin, and the incomparable grace of Jesus in spite of it, we are humbled and thankful. When telling the Lord you are thankful or praising Him feels too hard, start with His gracious and beautiful gospel. Recite what you know of His character. Here are a few prompts:

Because He is good, I give thanks.[101]
His love toward me never ceases; I give thanks[102].
His ways are not my ways; I give thanks[103].
He is kind, merciful, gracious, and patient; I give thanks.[104]

If I am grateful that His own beloved Son's death was for my good and accomplished *everything* for me,[105] then when I think of my daughter I can give thanks for her life (however brief) and her death (however much I grieve it). I don't have to fully understand the paradox of that sacrifice.[106] As we surrender to the Lord, He meets us in the offering. He comforts us in our confusion. He is working all of eternity toward His perfect will,[107] and when we see Him face to face, that will be answer enough.

Choosing to give thanks — and then doing so again and again until we have a heart inclined toward gratitude —serves as a safeguard for our faith. When we stop seeing God's activity and provision as gifts, our hearts yield to thoughts and feelings of entitlement and bitterness. We become myopic, overlooking the blessings around us as the thing we do not have grows in importance and consumes our affections, becoming an accidental idol that leaves us empty.[108] But as we reorient our hearts and minds to see what we do have —which we didn't earn or deserve — it realigns our souls toward rest. We rest as the beneficiaries of God's grace.

REFLECTION QUESTIONS

Do you find it easy or difficult to give thanks to the Lord now?

What are you thankful for today?

For further study: Psalm 103

DAY 5

$\mathcal{W}al\!k$: IN GRACE

And God is able to make all grace abound to you,
so that having all sufficiency in all things at all times,
you may abound in every good work.
- 2 Corinthians 9:8 -

"I don't know how to do this, God."

By "this" I meant living with grief. Learning to move forward (not "on"!) felt like a rebirth. I was adapting to a new life where nothing would ever be the same. But that didn't mean that it wouldn't be good again. David wrote in Psalm 27:13, "I believe that I shall look upon the goodness of the Lord in the land of the living!" As you and I are both still in the land of the living, that hope holds true for us. We shall see God's goodness. How? By grace.

The word "grace" has been summarized in a helpful acronym, "God's Riches At Christ's Expense". Meaning that in the humiliation and death of Jesus Christ,[109] we have been given all of God's fullness and riches.[110]

Christ, the Son of God, bore our punishment that we would be counted as sons and daughters of God.[111] Christ, the perfect atoning Lamb, took on our sin that we could be made righteous and holy.[112] Christ, who could not be held by death,[113] rose from the dead and gave hope of eternal joy[114] and life to those who would believe in His name.[115]

Our entrance into faith is solely by Christ's work for us – we added nothing to our salvation except our need for it. It was grace working for us that opened our eyes to a repentant faith.[116] In Romans 8, the apostle Paul argues that if God went to such great and costly lengths to save us by giving us Christ, how much more will He grant to us our daily needs?[117] For as long as we live and far into eternity, we will continue to unearth the gems of God's kindness and grace.

How is God's grace at work for those who are learning to live with grief? Grace is at work when you rise, filling your lungs with air and enabling your body to move. It's working in you as you push past the despair and choose to hope. Grace is at work, supplying you with faith to believe in God's character and promises, even when your circumstances scream loudly against Him. God's riches of patience, kindness, and gentleness are available to you when blindsided by a hard conversation or a thoughtless comment. God's fullness of peace is yours when you can't breathe for the sobbing and the lonely days ahead that stretch on and on. God's strength is enough to help you get through the long day at work. And when you lay your head down to sleep, you can rest knowing that God never does — He is always awake, alert, and working for your good. The only way through grief is by grace alone.

REFLECTION QUESTIONS

What evidences of grace can you see around you today?

How is God's saving grace through Jesus the answer to grief?

For further study: Ephesians 2

Meditate:

GREAT IS THY FAITHFULNESS

Great is Thy faithfulness,
O God my Father;
There is no shadow of turning with Thee.
Thou changest not,
Thy compassions they fail not,
As Thou hast been
Thou forever will be.

Great is Thy faithfulness!
Great is Thy faithfulness!
Morning by morning new mercies I see,
And all I have needed Thy hand hath provided
Great is Thy faithfulness,
Lord unto me.

Pardon for sin
And a peace that endureth,
Thine own dear presence to cheer
And to guide;
Strength for today
And bright hope for tomorrow,
Blessings all mine, with ten thousand beside.

Words by Thomas Chisholm (1923).

DAY 7

Journal: WEEK IN REVIEW

Look back over the devotions from this week. Which was most significant to you?

What aspect of walking with the Lord do you find easy to do? What do you find difficult?

What line(s) from the hymn did you find meaningful?

Write out one verse or verses of Scripture that impacted you this week.

A FINAL WORD OF ENCOURAGEMENT

Who stirred up one from the east
whom victory meets at every step?
- Isaiah 41:2a -

"Whom victory meets at every step..." that's a description of our Lord. There is no circumstance that makes Him falter or hesitate. No depth that He cannot handle, no depression He cannot lighten. There is no question that causes Him to stumble for an answer. There is no force or action or circumstance that could come against Him and win.

Life after grief may be overwhelming, dreary, and dark to us, but never to Christ. As we keep coming to Him one day at a time, beholding His beauty, finding comfort and strength in His character, and learning to walk through grief while being held by the One who never fails, He leads us in the way victorious.

Isaiah 41 goes on to say in verse 13, "For I, the LORD your God, hold your right hand; it is I who say to you, 'Fear not, I am the one who helps you.'" For us who are in Christ, the promise made to the nation of Israel has implications for us as well, since we have been grafted into their inheritance.[118]

The Lord is walking with us, holding our hand, helping us along. These lyrics sum it up well:

He will hold me fast,
He will hold me fast;
For my Savior loves me so,
He will hold me fast.[119]

ACKNOWLEDGEMENTS

To Cori Hennessee: thank you for the gift of editing, laughter, and excellent Facetime conversations regarding theology, mom-life, and rearranging furniture for the 108th time. My I-O-U count is up to at least 403.

To Constance Ray: from day one, your creative gift of graphic design has made me feel loved and seen. Thank you for knowing me, working with me, and willingly enduring all streams of consciousness feedback.

To Jennifer Parks: Thank you for allowing me the honor of writing for Hope Mommies. I am humbled and grateful to have you in my corner, and have loved watching God grow the ministry of HM in your gracious and wise hands! Soli Deo Gloria.

To Sarah, Holly, Lauren, and Rachel: I would choose a weekend with you women any day. You're fierce in your love, willing to do whatever it takes, and so incredibly fun. The overflow of joy in your service to Jesus has been an immeasurable blessing to me.

To Megan and Dustin: though you are holding about 13,000 of mine, I still do not have sufficient words to express to you both. It has been a heart wrenching and sacred honor to journey with you as you love and long for Blakelee. Watching God do again what He did for us (namely, demonstrate His faithful love that *will not let you go*) has deepened my faith and trust in His providence, wherever He may lead. Thank you for sharing your lives with me.

To Malacai and Gemma: you are my daily reminders of God's grace to me. I did nothing to earn or deserve the gifts of you both, but I am incredibly grateful! Thank you for praying for Mommy, letting Mommy work, and for loving God, Hope Mommies, Gwendolyn, and Baby C with such honest faith. "My heart is yours."

To Blair: thank you for seeing me, supporting me, and walking proudly with me. By grace we have made it on this grief pilgrimage for the past ten years; by grace we will keep moving until we're Home. I am thankful to be at your side on the journey.

Whatever it takes and wherever You lead, I am always in, Lord. You have and always will be enough.

ABOUT THE AUTHOR

Erin Cushman (B.A. University of North Texas) is the founder and former Executive Director of Hope Mommies, a gospel-centric nonprofit ministry that serves the infant loss community. She is the author of *Anchored: a Bible Study for Miscarriage, Stillbirth and Infant Loss*, and holds a certification in Biblical Counseling from Southwestern Baptist Theological Seminary in Fort Worth, Texas. She and her husband Blair, live in New Braunfels, Texas with their two living children.

ABOUT HOPE MOMMIES

Hope Mommies™ is a nonprofit organization sharing the hope of Christ with women who have experienced miscarriage, stillbirth and infant loss. Hope Mommies vision is that every woman would find a safe community to share their grief, and know the hope found in Jesus Christ who alone can heal and redeem their story. More information can be found at hopemommies.org, and @HopeMommies on Instagram, Twitter and Facebook.

ADDITIONAL RESOURCES

A Grief Observed, C.S. Lewis
Dark Clouds, Deep Mercy, Mark Voegrop
From Grief to Glory, James Bruce III
Hymns of Grace Pew Edition by the Masters Seminary; John MacArthur and various authors
The Valley of Vision: a Collection of Puritan Prayers and Devotions, Arthur Bennett
Safe in the Arms of God, John MacArthur
Hearing Jesus Speak Into Your Sorrow, Nancy Guthrie

ENDNOTES

COME

[1] Charles Spurgeon, *Morning and Evening* (September 13).

[2] Sandra McCracken, Hope Mommies annual retreat, Marble Falls, Texas, 2014. www.sandramccracken.com.

[3] "Therefore, since we are surrounded by so great a cloud of witnesses, let us also lay aside every weight, and sin which clings so closely, and let us run with endurance the race that is set before us." Hebrews 12:1

[4] "Let me hear in the morning of your steadfast love, for in you I trust. Make me know the way I should go, for to you I lift up my soul." Psalm 143:8

[5] "I will instruct you and teach you in the way you should go; I will counsel you with my eye upon you." Psalm 32:8

[6] "Because he inclined his ear to me, therefore I will call on him as long as I live." Psalm 116:2

[7] "How can I give you up, O Ephraim? How can I hand you over, O Israel? How can I make you like Admah? How can I treat you like Zeboiim? My heart recoils within me; my compassion grows warm and tender." Hosea 11:8

[8] "I will make with them an everlasting covenant, that I will not turn away from doing good to them. And I will put the fear of me in their hearts, that they may not turn from me." Jeremiah 32:40

[9] "For 'In him we live and move and have our being.'" Acts 17:28

[10] "The Lord looks down from heaven; he sees all the children of man; from where he sits enthroned he looks out on all the inhabitants of the earth he who fashions the hearts of them all and observes all their deeds." Psalm 33:13-15

[11] "For I am God, and there is no other; I am God, and there is none like me, declaring the end from the beginning and from ancient times things not yet done, saying, 'My counsel shall stand, and I will accomplish all my purpose.' Isaiah 46:9b-10

[12] "For he who sanctifies and those who are sanctified all have one source. That is why he is not ashamed to call them brothers, saying 'I will tell of your name to my brothers; in the midst of the congregation I will sing your praise.'" Hebrews 2:11-12

[13] "For the Lord is righteous; he loves righteous deeds; the upright shall behold his face." Psalm 11:7

[14] "But you do see, for you note mischief and vexation, that you may take it into your hands; to you the helpless commits himself; you have been the helper of the fatherless." Psalm 10:14

[15] "The LORD is near to the brokenhearted and saves the crushed in spirit." Psalm 34:18

[16] "And will not God give justice to his elect, who cry to him day and night? Will he delay long over them? I tell you, he will give justice to them speedily. Nevertheless, when the Son of Man comes, will he find faith on earth?" Luke 18:7-8

[17] "Hear, O Israel: The LORD our God, the LORD is one." Deuteronomy 6:4

[18] "In the beginning, God created the heavens and the earth." Genesis 1:1

[19] "Go therefore and make disciples of all nations, baptizing them in the name of the Father and of the Son and of the Holy Spirit, teaching them to observe all that I have commanded you. And behold, I am with you always, to the end of the age." Matthew 28:19-20

[20] "Have you not known? Have you not heard? The LORD is the everlasting God, the Creator of the ends of the earth. He does not faint or grow weary; his understanding is unsearchable." Isaiah 40:28

[21] "He is the radiance of the glory of God and the exact imprint of his nature, and he upholds the universe by the word of his power." Hebrews 1:3a

[22] "There is no fear in love, but perfect love casts out fear. For fear has to do with punishment, and whoever fears has not been perfected in love." 1 John 4:18

[23] "'The Rock, his work is perfect, for all his ways are justice. A God of faithfulness and without iniquity, just and upright is he.'" Deuteronomy 32:4

[24] "For his invisible attributes, namely, his eternal power and divine nature, have been clearly perceived, ever since the creation of the world, in the things that have been made. So they are without excuse." Romans 1:20

[25] "All Scripture is breathed out by God and profitable for teaching, for reproof, for correction, and for training in righteousness, that the man of God may be complete, equipped for every good work." 2 Timothy 3:16-17

[26] "He is the image of the invisible God, the firstborn of all creation." Colossians 1:15

[27] "I say to the LORD, 'You are my Lord; I have no good apart from you.'" Psalm 16:2

[28] "He has delivered us from the domain of darkness and transferred us to the kingdom of his beloved Son, in whom we have redemption, the forgiveness of sins." Colossians 1:13-14

[29] "'And behold, I am with you always, to the end of the age.'" Matthew 28:20b

[30] "But the fruit of the Spirit is love, joy, peace, patience, kindness, goodness, faithfulness, gentleness, self-control; against such things there is no law." Galatians 5:22-23

[31] And I heard a loud voice from the throne saying, "Behold, the dwelling place of God is with man. He will dwell with them, and they will be his people, and God himself will be with them as their God [4] He will wipe away every tear from their eyes, and death shall be no more, neither shall there be mourning, nor crying, nor pain anymore, for the former things have passed away." Revelation 21:3-4

BEHOLD
[32] VanGemeren, W. (Ed.). (1997). _New international dictionary of Old Testament theology & exegesis_ (Vol. 1, p. 1048). Grand Rapids, MI: Zondervan Publishing House.

[33] "I myself will be the shepherd of my sheep, and I myself will make them lie down, declares the Lord God. I will seek the lost, and I will bring back the strayed, and I will bind up the injured, and I will strengthen the weak, and the fat and the strong I will destroy. I will feed them in justice." Ezekiel 34:15-16

[34] "'I am the good shepherd. I know my own and my own know me.'" John 10:14

[35] "So I exhort the elders among you, as a fellow elder and a witness of the sufferings of Christ, as well as a partaker in the glory that is going to be revealed: shepherd the flock of God that is among you, exercising oversight, not under compulsion, but willingly, as God would have you; not for shameful gain, but eagerly; not domineering over those in your charge, but being examples to the flock. And when the chief Shepherd appears, you will receive the unfading crown of glory." 1 Peter 5:1-4

[36] "The next day he saw Jesus coming toward him, and said, 'Behold, the Lamb of God, who takes away the sin of the world!'" John 1:29

[37] "But every nation still made gods of its own and put them in the shrines of the high places that the Samaritans had made, every nation in the cities in which they lived." 2 Kings 17:29

[38] Dorman, Peter F., and John R. Baines. "The Gods." Encyclopædia Britannica, Encyclopædia Britannica, Inc., 10 Oct. 2017, www.britannica.com/topic/ancient-Egyptian-religion/The-Gods.

[39] "And he is before all things, and in him all things hold together." Colossians 1:17

[40] "Therefore, just as sin came into the world through one man, and death through sin, and so death spread to all men because all sinned— for sin indeed was in the world before the law was given, but sin is not counted where there is no law. Yet death reigned from Adam to Moses, even over those whose sinning was not like the transgression of Adam, who was a type of the one who was to come." Romans 5:12-14

[41] "For all have sinned and fall short of the glory of God, and are justified by his grace as a gift, through the redemption that is in Christ Jesus." Romans 3:23-24

[42] "And I will give you a new heart, and a new spirit I will put within you. And I will remove the heart of stone from your flesh and give you a heart of flesh. And I will put my Spirit within you, and cause you to walk in my statutes and be careful to obey my rules." Ezekiel 36:26-27

[43] "'Whoever believes in the Son has eternal life; whoever does not obey the Son shall not see life, but the wrath of God remains on him.'" John 3:36

[44] "This poor man cried, and the LORD heard him and saved him out of all his troubles." Psalm 34:6

[45] "'In my Father's house are many rooms. If it were not so, would I have told you that I go to prepare a place for you? And if I go and prepare a place for you, I will come again and will take you to myself, that where I am you may be also.'" John 14:2-3

[46] "Consequently, he is able to save to the uttermost those who draw near to God through him, since he always lives to make intercession for them." Hebrews 7:25

[47] "'Nevertheless, I tell you the truth: it is to your advantage that I go away, for if I do not go away, the Helper will not come to you. But if I go, I will send him to you. And when he comes, he will convict the world concerning sin and righteousness and judgment.'" John 16:7-8

[48] And we all, with unveiled face, beholding the glory of the Lord, are being transformed into the same image from one degree of glory to another. For this comes from the Lord who is the Spirit. 2 Corinthians 3:18

[49] "'It is the LORD who goes before you. He will be with you; he will not leave you or forsake you. Do not fear or be dismayed.'" Deuteronomy 31:8

[50] "…that the God of our Lord Jesus Christ, the Father of glory, may give you the Spirit of wisdom and of revelation in the knowledge of him," Ephesians 1:17

[51] "May the God of hope fill you with all joy and peace in believing, so that by the power of the Holy Spirit you may abound in hope." Romans 15:13

FIND

[52] "Jesus Christ is the same yesterday and today and forever." Hebrews 13:8

[53] "'Ask, and it will be given to you; seek, and you will find; knock, and it will be opened to you.'" Matthew 7:7

[54] "He who dwells in the shelter of the Most High will abide in the shadow of the Almighty; He will cover you with his pinions, and under his wings you will find refuge; his faithfulness is a shield and buckler." Psalm 91:1,4

[55] "The man gave names to all livestock and to the birds of the heavens and to every beast of the field. But for Adam there was not found a helper fit for him." Genesis 2:20

[56] Credit for understanding the difference between transparency and vulnerability go to Dr. Garrett Higbee and Lee Lewis, biblical counselors that serve with the Great Commission Collective.

[57] "GOD, the Lord, is my strength; he makes my feet like the deer's; he makes me tread on my high places. To the choirmaster: with stringed instruments." Habakkuk 3:19

[58] "Lamentations." An Introduction to the Old Testament, by Tremper Longman and Raymond B. Dollard, Zondervan, 2007, pp. 344.

[59] "After these things the word of the LORD came to Abram in a vision: 'Fear not, Abram, I am your shield; your reward shall be very great.'" Genesis 15:1

[60] "...so that by two unchangeable things, in which it is impossible for God to lie, we who have fled for refuge might have strong encouragement to hold fast to the hope set before us." Hebrews 6:18

[61] "Who shall separate us from the love of Christ? Shall tribulation, or distress, or persecution, or famine, or nakedness, or danger, or sword?" Romans 8:25

[62] "'Have I not commanded you? Be strong and courageous. Do not be frightened, and do not be dismayed, for the LORD your God is with you wherever you go.'" Joshua 1:9

[63] "'Is anything too hard for the LORD?'" Genesis 18:14a

[64] "The LORD passed before him and proclaimed, 'The LORD, the LORD, a God merciful and gracious, slow to anger, and abounding in steadfast love and faithfulness...'" Exodus 34:6

[65] "A bruised reed he will not break, and a faintly burning wick he will not quench, he will faithfully bring forth justice." Isaiah 42:3

[66] "I, wisdom, dwell with prudence, and I find knowledge and discretion; the LORD possessed me at the beginning of this work, the first of his acts of old." Proverbs 8:12, 22

[67] "The sum of your word is truth, and every one of your righteous rules endures forever." Psalm 119:160

[68] "Bless the LORD, O my soul, and forget not all his benefits, who forgives all your iniquity, who heals all your diseases, who redeems your life from the pit, who crowns you with steadfast love and mercy." Psalm 103:2-4

[69] "He does not deal with us according to our sins, nor repay us according to our iniquities." Psalm 103:10

[70] "'I know that you can do all things, and that no purpose of yours can be thwarted. "Who is this that hides counsel without knowledge?" Therefore I have uttered what I did not understand, things too wonderful for me, which I did not know.'" Job 42:2-3

[71] "'For I know the plans I have for you, declares the LORD, plans for welfare and not for evil, to give you a future and a hope. Then you will call upon me and come and pray to me, and I will hear you.'" Jeremiah 29:11-12

WALK

[72] "'And I will lead the blind in a way that they do not know in paths that they have not known I will guide them. I will turn the darkness before them into light, the rough places into level ground. These are the things I do, and I do not forsake them.'" Isaiah 42:16

[73] "Every good gift and every perfect gift is from above, coming down from the Father of lights, with whom there is no variation or shadow due to change." James 1:17

[74] "For I am sure that neither death nor life, nor angels nor rulers, nor things present nor things to come, nor powers, nor height nor depth, nor anything else in all creation, will be able to separate us from the love of God in Christ Jesus our Lord." Romans 8:38-39

[75] "You are good and do good; teach me your statutes." Psalm 119:68

[76] "The steadfast love of the LORD never ceases; his mercies never come to an end; they are new every morning; great is your faithfulness." Lamentations 3:22-23

[77] "Indeed, none who wait for you shall be put to shame; they shall be ashamed who are wantonly treacherous." Psalm 25:3

[78] "Therefore, just as sin came into the world through one man, and death through sin, and so death spread to all men because all sinned…" Romans 5:12

[79] "For to us a child is born, to us a son is given; and the government shall be upon his shoulder, and his name shall be called Wonderful Counselor, Mighty God, Everlasting Father, Prince of Peace." Isaiah 9:6

[80] "Do not be anxious about anything, but in everything by prayer and supplication with thanksgiving let your requests be made known to God. And the peace of God, which surpasses all understanding, will guard your hearts and your minds in Christ Jesus." Philippians 4:6-7

[81] "You keep him in perfect peace whose mind is stayed on you, because he trusts in you. Trust in the Lord forever, for the Lord God is an everlasting rock." Isaiah 26:3-4

[82] "May the God of hope fill you with all joy and peace in believing, so that by the power of the Holy Spirit you may abound in hope." Romans 15:13

[83] "'Incline your ear, and come to me; hear, that your soul may live; and I will make with you an everlasting covenant, my steadfast, sure love for David.'" Isaiah 55:3

[84] Bob Kellemen. "The Beauty of Our Emotions." *Biblical Counseling Coalition,* 20 July 2020. www.biblicalcounselingcoalition.org/2020/07/20/the-beauty-of-our-emotions/.

[85] "The Lord your God is in your midst, a mighty one who will save; he will rejoice over you with gladness; he will quiet you by his love; he will exult over you with loud singing." Zephaniah 3:17

[86] "And do not grieve the Holy Spirit of God, by whom you were sealed for the day of redemption." Ephesians 4:30

[87] "And they were bringing children to him that he might touch them, and the disciples rebuked them. But when Jesus saw it, he was indignant and said to them, 'Let the children come to me; do not hinder them, for to such belongs the kingdom of God.'" Mark 10:13-14

[88] "He who sits in the heavens laughs; the Lord holds them in derision." Psalm 2:4

[89] "Trust in him at all times, O people; pour out your heart before him; God is a refuge for us. Selah" Psalm 62:8

[90] "I cry out to God Most High, to God who fulfills his purpose for me." Psalm 57:2

[91] "He will cover you with his pinions, and under his wings you will find refuge; his faithfulness is a shield and buckler." Psalm 91:4

[92] "I sought the Lord, and he answered me and delivered me from all my fears." Psalm 34:4

[93] "Casting all your anxieties on him, because he cares for you." 1 Peter 5:7

[94] "So we have come to know and to believe the love that God has for us. God is love, and whoever abides in love abides in God, and God abides in him." 1 John 4:16

[95] "Looking to Jesus, the founder and perfecter of our faith, who for the joy that was set before him endured the cross, despising the shame, and is seated

at the right hand of the throne of God. Consider him who endured from sinners such hostility against himself, so that you may not grow weary or fainthearted." Hebrews 12:2-3

[96] "Put on then, as God's chosen ones, holy and beloved, compassionate hearts, kindness, humility, meekness, and patience, [13] bearing with one another and, if one has a complaint against another, forgiving each other; as the Lord has forgiven you, so you also must forgive. [14] And above all these put on love, which binds everything together in perfect harmony." Colossians 3:12-14

[97] "If possible, so far as it depends on you, live peaceably with all." Romans 12:18

[98] "'For if you forgive others their trespasses, your heavenly Father will also forgive you, but if you do not forgive others their trespasses, neither will your Father forgive your trespasses.'" Matthew 6:14-15

[99] "Through him then let us continually offer up a sacrifice of praise to God, that is, the fruit of lips that acknowledge his name." Hebrews 13:15

[100] "But the king said to Araunah, 'No, but I will buy it from you for a price. I will not offer burnt offerings to the Lord my God that cost me nothing.' So David bought the threshing floor and the oxen for fifty shekels of silver." 2 Samuel 24:24

[101] "Oh give thanks to the LORD, for he is good; for his steadfast love endures forever!" 1 Chronicles 16:34

[102] "Give thanks to the Lord of lords, for his steadfast love endures forever." Psalm 136:3

[103] "For as the heavens are higher than the earth, so are my ways higher than your ways and my thoughts than your thoughts." Isaiah 55:9

[104] "The LORD descended in the cloud and stood with him there, and proclaimed the name of the LORD. The LORD passed before him and

proclaimed, "The LORD, the LORD, a God merciful and gracious, slow to anger, and abounding in steadfast love and faithfulness," Exodus 34:5-6

[105] "He who did not spare his own Son but gave him up for us all, how will he not also with him graciously give us all things?" Romans 8:32

[106] "For as the heavens are higher than the earth, so are my ways higher than your ways and my thoughts than your thoughts." Isaiah 55:9

[107] "For I consider that the sufferings of this present time are not worth comparing with the glory that is to be revealed to us. For the creation waits with eager longing for the revealing of the songs of God." Romans 8:18-19

[108] "He feeds on ashes; a deluded heart has led him astray, and he cannot deliver himself or say, 'Is there not a lie in my right hand?'" Isaiah 44:20

[109] "Who, though he was in the form of God, did not count equality with God a thing to be grasped, but emptied himself, by taking the form of a servant, being born in the likeness of men. And being found in human form, he humbled himself by becoming obedient to the point of death, even death on a cross." Philippians 2:6-8

[110] "and to know the love of Christ that surpasses knowledge, that you may be filled with all the fullness of God." Ephesians 3:19

[111] "But when the fullness of time had come, God sent forth his Son, born of woman, born under the law, to redeem those who were under the law, so that we might receive adoption as sons. And because you are sons, God has sent the Spirit of his Son into our hearts, crying, 'Abba! Father!' So you are no longer a slave, but a son, and if a son, then an heir through God." Galatians 4:4-7

[112] "He predestined us for adoption to himself as sons through Jesus Christ, according to the purpose of his will, to the praise of his glorious grace, with which he has blessed us in the Beloved. In him we have redemption through his blood, the forgiveness of our

trespasses, according to the riches of his grace, which he lavished upon us, in all wisdom and insight." Ephesians 1:5-8

[113] "This Jesus, delivered up according to the definite plan and foreknowledge of God, you crucified and killed by the hands of lawless men. God raised him up, loosing the pangs of death, because it was not possible for him to be held by it." Acts 2:23-24

[114] "And the ransomed of the Lord shall return and come to Zion with singing everlasting joy shall be upon their heads; they shall obtain gladness and joy, and sorrow and sighing shall flee away." Isaiah 51:11

[115] "'For this is the will of my Father, that everyone who looks on the Son and believes in him should have eternal life, and I will raise him up on the last day.'" John 6:40

[116] "For by grace you have been saved through faith. And this is not your own doing; it is the gift of God, not a result of works, so that no one may boast." Ephesians 2:8-9

[117] "What then shall we say to these things? If God is for us, who can be against us? He who did not spare his own Son but gave him up for us all, how will he not also with him graciously give us all things?" Romans 8:31-32

[118] "But if some of the branches were broken off, and you, although a wild olive shoot, were grafted in among the others and now share in the nourishing root[s] of the olive tree, [18] do not be arrogant toward the branches. If you are, remember it is not you who support the root, but the root that supports you. [19] Then you will say, "Branches were broken off so that I might be grafted in." [20] That is true. They were broken off because of their unbelief, but you stand fast through faith. So do not become proud, but fear." Romans 11:17-20

[119] Words by Ada R. Habershon (1908).

Made in the USA
Monee, IL
08 May 2021